Ecstasy
Dangerous Euphoria

ILLICIT AND MISUSED DRUGS

ILLICIT AND MISUSED DRUGS

Ecstasy
Dangerous Euphoria

by Malinda Miller

Mason Crest

Mason Crest
370 Reed Road
Broomall, Pennsylvania 19008
www.masoncrest.com

Printed in the Hashemite Kingdom of Jordan.

First printing
9 8 7 6 5 4 3 2 1

Library of Congress Cataloging-in-Publication Data

Miller, Malinda, 1979-
Ecstasy : dangerous euphoria / by Malinda Miller.
    p. cm. — (Illicit and misused drugs)
ISBN 978-1-4222-2431-1 (hardcover)
ISBN 978-1-4222-2424-3 (hardcover series)
ISBN 978-1-4222-2450-2 (paperback)
ISBN 978-1-4222-9295-2 (ebook)
1. Ecstasy (Drug)—Juvenile literature. 2. Drug abuse—Juvenile literature. I. Title.
  HV5822.M38M55 2012
  362.29'9—dc22
                                        2011004340

Interior design by Benjamin Stewart.
Cover design by Torque Advertising + Design.
Produced by Harding House Publishing Services, Inc.
www.hardinghousepages.com

CONTENTS

INTRODUCTION

Addicting drugs are among the greatest challenges to health, well-being, and the sense of independence and freedom for which we all strive—and yet these drugs are present in the everyday lives of most people. Almost every home has alcohol or tobacco waiting to be used, and has medicine cabinets stocked with possibly outdated but still potentially deadly drugs. Almost everyone has a friend or loved one with an addiction-related problem. Almost everyone seems to have a solution neatly summarized by word or phrase: medicalization, legalization, criminalization, war-on-drugs.

For better and for worse, drug information seems to be everywhere, but what information sources can you trust? How do you separate misinformation (whether deliberate or born of ignorance and prejudice) from the facts? Are prescription drugs safer than "street" drugs? Is occasional drug use really harmful? Is cigarette smoking more addictive than heroin? Is marijuana safer than alcohol? Are the harms caused by drug use limited to the users? Can some people become addicted following just a few exposures? Is treatment or counseling just for those with serious addiction problems?

These are just a few of the many questions addressed in this series. It is an empowering series because it provides the information and perspectives that can help people come to their own opinions and find answers to the challenges posed by drugs in their own lives. The series also provides further resources for information and assistance, recognizing that no single source has all the answers. It should be of interest and relevance to areas of study spanning biology, chemistry, history, health, social studies and more. Its efforts to provide a real-world context for the information that is clearly presented but not overly simplified should be appreciated by students, teachers, and parents.

The series is especially commendable in that it does not pretend to pose easy answers or imply that all decisions can be made on the basis of simple facts: some challenges have no immediate or simple solutions, and some solutions will need to rely as much upon basic values as basic facts. Despite this, the series should help to at least provide a foundation of knowledge. In the end, it may help as much by pointing out where the solutions are not simple, obvious, or known to work. In fact, at many points, the reader is challenged to think for him- or herself by being asked what his or her opinion is.

A core concept of the series is to recognize that we will never have all the facts, and many of the decisions will never be easy. Hopefully, however, armed with information, perspective, and resources, readers will be better prepared for taking on the challenges posed by addictive drugs in everyday life.

— *Jack E. Henningfield, Ph.D.*

7 What Is Ecstasy?

Daniel wanted his prom night to be special. Before leaving for the dance, he took some colorful pills stamped with fun images. They looked like harmless candy, but Daniel found out how dangerous they were.

"My heart was racing so fast. I thought I was having a heart attack," Daniel said. A friend had to help him to the prom because his legs were shaking so badly. After arriving at the location of the dance, a Hollywood movie set, Daniel started to feel better.

"Then I hit a peak," he said. "I felt like a movie star."

After the dance, at a friend's house, Daniel crashed down to a low. He felt depressed and confused. Trying to recover his high, he swallowed two more candy-like pills.

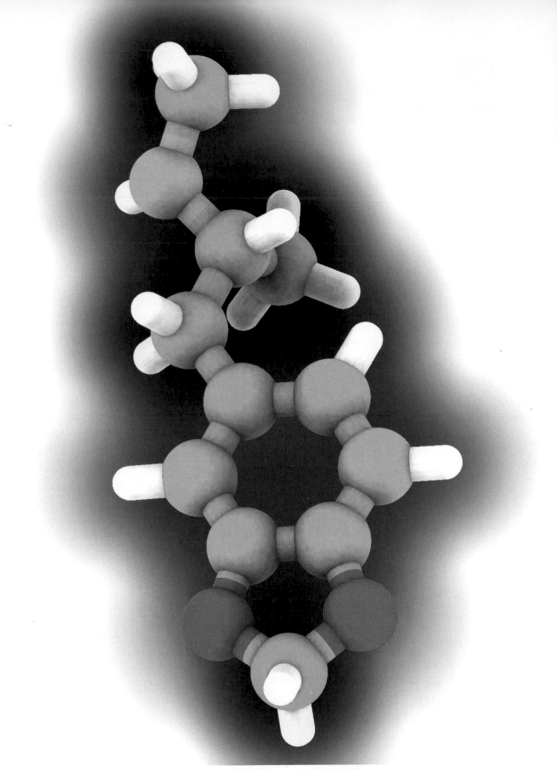

A chemical model of an MDMA molecule, from which ecstasy is composed.

"I laid down on the bed for a few minutes and couldn't lift my head," he said. "My legs were rocking back and forth."

Daniel's story, adapted from a true story at the National Institute on Drug Abuse for Teens website (teens.drugabuse.gov/stories/story_xtc1.php), describes the highs and the lows of a young man's first experience using the illicit drug ecstasy.

What Is Ecstasy?

Ecstasy is the common name for the chemical 3,4 methylenedioxymethamphetamine, or MDMA. Other chemicals are sometimes sold as ecstasy, but for the purposes of this book we will be talking about MDMA, a synthetic, or man-made, drug that is a stimulant as well as a hallucinogen. The stimulant properties of MDMA cause feelings of increased energy and euphoria in the user, while the hallucinogenic properties of the chemical can result in dis-

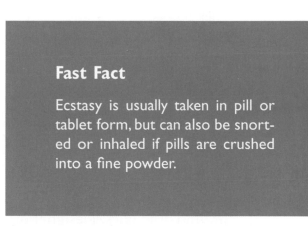

Fast Fact

Ecstasy is usually taken in pill or tablet form, but can also be snorted or inhaled if pills are crushed into a fine powder.

tortions in time, perception, and touch. Ecstasy is also sometimes called an empathogen or entactogen, both terms that refer to the drug's ability to induce feelings of *empathy* in the user.

Ecstasy is a designer drug—a drug created by slightly altering the molecule of an existing drug in order to get

Drug Classifications

Drugs, both illicit and prescribed, fall into certain classifications depending on how they are used or how they affect the body.

- Stimulants speed up the body and the brain, increasing energy and alertness. Stimulants include ecstasy, amphetamines, caffeine, nicotine, and cocaine.
- Depressants slow down the body's normal activity by relaxing muscles and lowering brain activity. Opioids, alcohol, barbiturates, tranquilizers, and benzodiazepines are all depressants, or "downers."
- Hallucinogens, also known as psychedelics, are mood-altering drugs that affect the brain, and make the user see, feel, or hear things that are not really there. Hallucinogens include LSD and PCP. Ecstasy can also act as a hallucinogen.
- Marijuana, the most commonly used illicit drug, causes a variety of psycho-active effects so that it does not fit neatly into one drug category.
- Inhalants are drugs that are breathed in through the mouth or nose in gas-eous form. They include many common household items such as gasoline, glue, and lighter fluid, among others.
- Antipsychotics are prescription drugs given to people who have mental conditions that cause delusions or hallucinations. Conditions commonly treated with antipsychotic medications include schizophrenia, bipolar dis-order, delusional disorder, and psychotic depression.
- Antidepressants are prescribed for people coping with depression. There are a number of different varieties of antidepressants, including selective serotonin reuptake inhibitors (SSRIs) and monoamine oxidase inhibitors (MAOIs).

around drug laws. Designer drugs are often created specifically to cause a high, especially one that simulates the high from another illicit drug. Though MDMA is a modification of an amphetamine molecule, and has similar properties to *methamphetamine*, it was originally created accidentally from the compound methylhydrastinine.

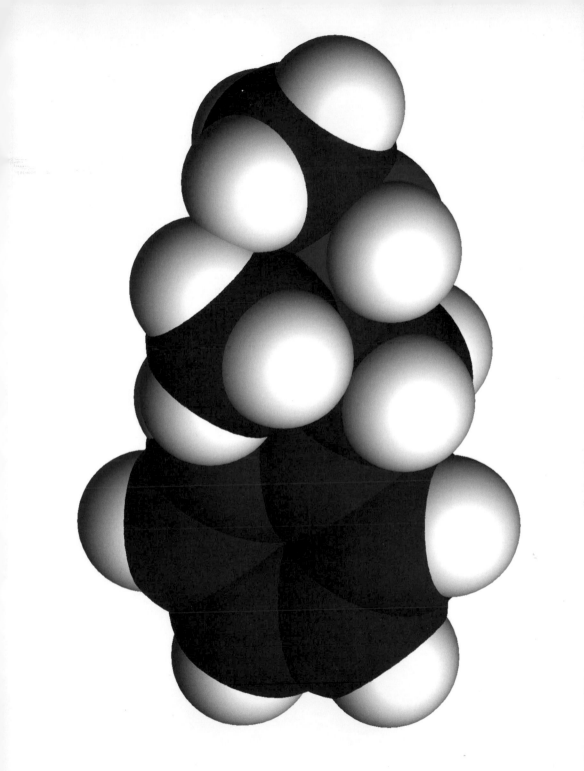

A molecule of methamphetamine looks—and acts—a little like ecstasy.

MDMA first became popular at rave parties in the 1970s and 1980s.

14 Chapter 1—What Is Ecstasy?

The scientist who created MDMA was trying to create a drug to stop or slow bleeding. MDMA was just an accidental middle product that was created during the process. MDMA was originally studied for possible medical use, but during the 1970s and 1980s it gained popularity as a recreational "club" drug, especially at nightclubs and *raves*, until the United States Drug Enforcement Administration (DEA) classified it as an illegal substance in 1985.

The quality of ecstasy pills varies drastically from pill to pill. Since it is an illegal substance, there are no regulations governing its manufacture. Therefore, the pill you buy as "ecstasy" may in fact be a number of chemicals. MDMA is the most common, and it is the one people want to take when they take ecstasy. Other chemicals that are sold as ecstasy include MDEA (3,4-Methylenedioxy-N-ethylamphetamine) and MDA (3,4-Methylenedioxy-amphetamine), both of which are drugs very chemically similar to MDMA and produce similar effects. Ecstasy pills may also be laced with a number of other substances, ranging from fairly *innocuous* like aspirin, to more dangerous and potentially lethal chemicals, like para-Methoxyamphetamine (PMA), a drug that has been linked to a number of ecstasy-related deaths.

Fast Fact

In the past, designer drugs could be created and sold legally because drug laws were written for specific drugs. The current drug laws have closed this loophole so that designer drugs can no longer be created without fear of prosecution.

What Does Ecstasy Do?

Ecstasy affects the brain by changing the chemicals that allow nerve cells in the brain to communicate with one another. Animal research has found that MDMA can be toxic to nerve cells and can cause long-lasting damage to them. MDMA also raises body temperature, which can have serious consequences, including death. Finally, ecstasy causes increased heart rate and blood pressure, which can also lead to serious medical problems.

Fast Fact

MDMA is derived from an essential oil of the sassafras tree.

Who Uses Ecstasy?

Ecstasy first became popular at nightclubs and raves, earning its reputation as a party or club drug. The teens and young adults at the raves would take ecstasy to keep partying all night long. Ecstasy is still mainly a club drug, but it is also used in private homes and on college campuses. Abuse of ecstasy is highest in the sixteen to twenty-five year-old age group, but use of the drug is not limited to only one age group.

Studies also show that ecstasy use is spreading from white youth to a broader range of ethnic groups. For example, in Chicago and New York, the drug continues to be mostly used by white young adults, but there are increasing reports of its distribution and use by African-American adults in their twenties and thirties.

Other research shows that ecstasy has also become a popular drug among urban gay males. This is especially

Ecstasy allows young adults to keep partying all night without getting tired.

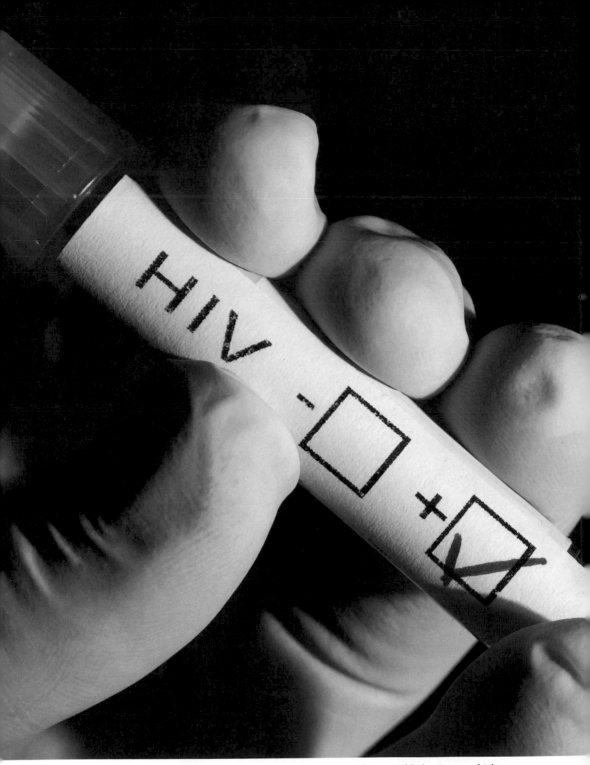

People who use ecstasy are more apt to engage in risky sexual behaviors—which in turn puts them at greater risk of getting HIV, the virus that causes AIDS.

18   Chapter 1—What Is Ecstasy?

Monitoring the Future

Since 1975, the Monitoring the Future (MTF) survey has measured drug, alcohol, and cigarette use and related attitudes among adolescent students nationwide. Survey participants report their drug-use behaviors across three time periods: lifetime, past year, and past month. In 2011, over 46,000 students in grades 8, 10, and 12 from 400 public and private schools participated in the survey. The survey is funded by the National Institute on Drug Abuse, a component of the National Institutes of Health, and conducted by the University of Michigan.

dangerous because club drugs have been linked to high-risk sexual behaviors that may lead to HIV or other sexually transmitted diseases. Many gay males in big cities report using ecstasy along with other drugs, including alcohol, marijuana, cocaine, methamphetamine, and ketamine.

Abuse of ecstasy reached a peak in 2000 and 2001, after which use fell sharply. However, the 2011 Monitoring the Future Study found that current and past-year use of MDMA has again risen among eighth and tenth graders. The MTF Survey found that in the year leading up to the survey, 1.7 percent of eighth-grade students, 4.5 percent of tenth-grade students, and 5.3 percent of twelfth-grade students had used ecstasy in the past year.

The 2010 National Survey on Drug Use and Health (NSDUH) also studied the trends of ecstasy use. In 2010, an estimated 695,000 people (0.3 percent of the population) in the United States ages twelve or older used ecstasy in the month prior to being surveyed. Approximately 937,000 Americans used ecstasy for the first time in 2010, which is a significant increase from the 894,000 first-time users reported in 2008. The average age that people started using ecstasy was 19.4 years old.

Why Do People Take Ecstasy?

People take ecstasy for its mood-altering effects. Ecstasy is considered a social drug, or a party drug, because it makes the user more relaxed in social situations. Ecstasy is supposed to make a fun experience more fun, and allow the user to keep partying all night long. Like alcohol, another "social lubricant," many users take ecstasy because it decreases *inhibitions*. Take, for example, this description of a first experience with ecstasy from the site www.ecstasy.org:

> Throughout my life I have always been one of the quiet ones. Shy, underconfident, insecure and introverted. . . .Guided by my 3 closest friends that night, I popped the Dove I was given and finally realized exactly who, and what I am. At the party, which we then went to, I soared! I met literally dozens of like-minded people, many of whom have now become very close friends and I talked and danced into the following morning, amazed that anything could feel so incredibly true. Until that night, I never knew that I could ever feel THAT good, that content, that in love with the world.

Like any drug, however, along with the "positive" effects of the high come many negative ones. MDMA can affect the body very quickly, which can be scary for the user and cause panic attacks. The drug's initial effects can also include nausea and confusion. While high on

Feeling socially awkward is common during adolescence. Some young adults with these feelings may feel that ecstasy offers them an easy way to overcome their natural shyness.

ecstasy, the user's thought processes are affected, meaning she might do something she normally would avoid. This loss of inhibitions is thought to be part of the "positive" social aspect of the drug, but it can also lead to negative consequences. For example, many ecstasy users make risky sexual choices, which can lead to pregnancy or sexually transmitted diseases.

An ecstasy high is often followed by a "crash"; users can feel depressed and tired for days after taking the drug. This crash also entices many users to immediately seek another high, either from more ecstasy or from another drug. Taking multiple doses of any drug is dangerous, but with ecstasy, "stacking," or doubling the dose, carries an especially high risk. The level of ecstasy builds and the user's body can't keep up with the amount of drug in his or her blood. That's what happened to Daniel at the beginning of this chapter.

Daniel's story exemplifies another risk of doing ecstasy: that it will lead to further experimentation with illicit drugs. In Daniel's case, his experiences with illicit drugs did not stop after his prom night. He became addicted to ecstasy and began dealing it and other drugs to pay for his habit. Daniel's one night of ecstasy turned into day after day of desperation and destruction until he faced homelessness.

Street Names for Cocaine Powder

E

X

XTC

rolls

Adam

hug

love drug

beans

clarity

lover's speed

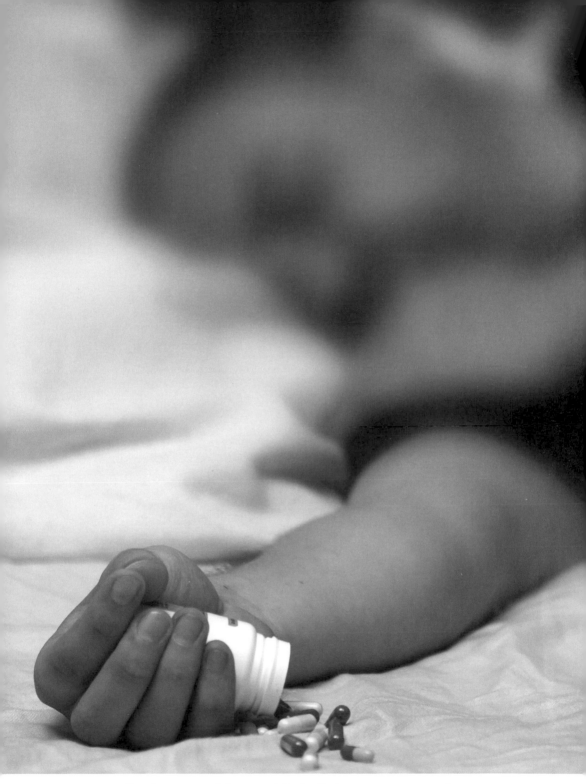

Overdose is one of the potentially deadly dangers ecstasy users face.

Life on the streets is about as far as you can get from the excitement and thrill of a rave—and yet ecstasy use can take you both places.

24   Chapter 1—What Is Ecstasy?

When he realized he was facing a life on the streets, Daniel turned his life around. Not everyone who uses ecstasy is so lucky. So just how did this dangerous drug become such a commonly used designer drug?

2 The History of Ecstasy

Many different stories have been invented about the origin of ecstasy. The most popular story claims that the German drug company Merck created MDMA in the early twentieth century as a diet pill. The company stopped use of the drug after a lot of funny side effects were observed in the test subjects. Along this same line, another myth says that MDMA pills were distributed to German troops during World War I to give the soldiers increased energy and reduce their need to eat. As this tales goes, the ecstasy pills also reduced the soldiers' drive to fight, leading to impromptu parties hosted in **No Man's Land** at Christmastime in 1914, during which German and British soldiers mingled, sang carols, and exchanged Christmas gifts. In fact, there *were* some ceasefires around Christmas during World War I, but they were *not* fueled by ecstasy.

Merck's old and established history alongside its place in the modern pharmaceutical world is easily seen in these two structure within its German headquarters. Ecstasy was first born here at the German pharmaceutical giant.

The Origin of Ecstasy

The truth about MDMA was hard to tease out from the myths about it because for a long time no one really knew how or why the drug was developed. The false stories were circulated as fact, even by normally reputable sources like scholarly articles, textbooks, and government websites. Finally, in 2006, the story was set straight when Roland W. Freudenmann (a professor of psychiatry), Florian Öxler, and Sabine Bernschneider-Reif (both from Merck's Department of Corporate History) searched Merck's archives and published an article revealing the results of their research. Freudenmann, Öxler, and Bernschneider-Reif credit a student, Christian Beck, with the original idea of searching the Merck archives for information about MDMA.

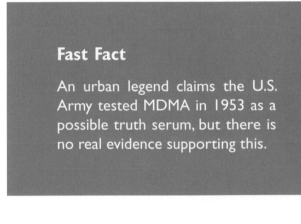

Fast Fact

An urban legend claims the U.S. Army tested MDMA in 1953 as a possible truth serum, but there is no real evidence supporting this.

The article reports that MDMA was first *synthesized* "as early as 1912," when its first mention can be found in a patent and a laboratory report. It turns out that the scientists who discovered the MDMA molecule were actually trying to create a blood-clotting drug similar to one already being sold by their competitor, Bayer. During their work, these scientists happened upon another chemical, which they named methylsafrylamin and added to the patent. Methylsafrylamin was listed only by its chemical formula, and was not deemed to be of any direct *therapeutic* value. It was only important as an intermediate product to making useful drugs; Merck patented the molecule, and all the chemical reactions around it.

Through the twentieth century, the chemical was tested a few times to see if it had any useful *pharmacological* properties. In 1927 it was tested in comparison with other stimulants, and found to have similar effects but to be more toxic than the other chemicals. The studies done on it in 1952 also found it to be a toxic substance. In 1959, it was resynthesized for the first time by Dr. Wolfgang Fruhstorfer, a chemist at Merck who was trying to produce new stimulants. The first paper specifically mentioning MDMA was published in 1960.

Modern Studies

Up until the 1960s, studies of the MDMA molecule had one thing in common—none of them found any medicinal value in the substance. In fact, it does not seem like the drug was tested on humans in any of the early studies, though reports from Dr. Fruhstorfer's 1959 studies are unclear on this point. In any case, MDMA was not considered even possible for any type of medicinal therapy (or for use as an illicit drug) until a man sometimes called a "psychonaut" started studying it.

The compound first invented by Merck was named methylsafrylamin, because it was made from the methyl oils of sassafras leaves.

Alexander Shulgin started his career innocently enough: he graduated from the University of California at Berkeley with a Ph.D. in biochemistry and went to work as a research chemist with Dow Chemical. Dow was happy with an insecticide Shulgin created, but his other research projects into psychedelic chemicals became a problem, until he was forced to leave Dow.

After leaving Dow, Shulgin continued to research new *psychoactive* chemicals. In 1976, he synthesized and tested MDMA. MDMA was only one of hundreds of psychoactive drugs he created and tested, but it is the one that he thought was most promising for use as a therapeutic drug.

In 1977, Shulgin shared some MDMA with Leo Zeff, a friend who was a psychologist. Zeff began treating some of his patients with MDMA. It was Zeff who coined the term "ADAM" because he claimed that the drug helped his patients regain their "*primordial* innocence." He introduced other therapists to MDMA, so that by the mid-1980s, the drug, which was still legal, was known as a valuable tool in experimental therapy.

MDMA Becomes Ecstasy

While the therapeutic uses of MDMA were growing, the street use of MDMA was also increasing.

Alexander Shulgin was the first to find a therapeutic use for MDMA.

The DEA is the part of the U.S. government that enforces drug-related laws.

Fast Fact

Alexander Shulgin created hundreds of psychedelic compounds—and tested almost all of them on himself.

In Dallas, Michael Clegg, a former seminary student, renamed the drug ecstasy and began selling it at nightclubs. Use increased rapidly among Dallas residents to as many as 30,000 hits of ecstasy per month. As a result, in 1985, the U.S. Department of Justice Drug Enforcement Administration (DEA) placed an emergency ban on MDMA as a Schedule I drug, corresponding to other chemicals with "no currently accepted medical use in treatment in the United States" and a "high potential for abuse."

After the DEA placed its emergency Schedule I status on ecstasy, a group of doctors and researchers sued the DEA to prevent the drug being permanently classified as a Schedule I drug. A court hearing was held, with one side arguing that MDMA caused brain damage in rats, and the other side claiming that the drug had therapeutic benefits for humans. The judge for the trial recommended that MDMA be placed on Schedule III, which would have allowed it to be manufactured, used by prescription, and subject to further research. Despite the judge's recommendation, the DEA decided to place

Fast Fact

In 1985, daytime talk-show host Phil Donahue devoted an entire episode of his show to the medical potential of MDMA.

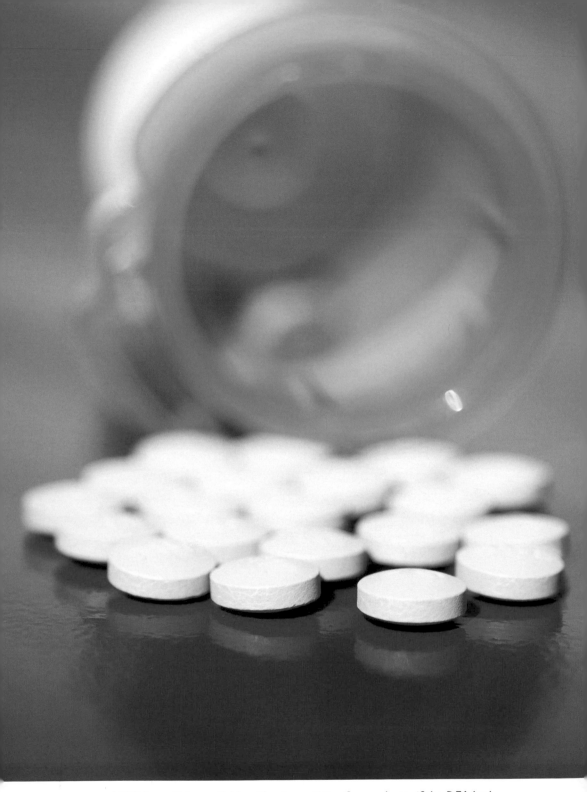

MDMA would be available with a prescription from a doctor if the DEA had placed the drug on the Schedule III list.

MDMA permanently on Schedule I. There has continued to be controversy surrounding this decision (which will be discussed in chapter 5).

U.S. Department of Justice Drug Enforcement Administration Drug Scheduling

Schedule I

• The drug or other substance has a high potential for abuse.
• The drug or other substance has no currently accepted medical use in treatment in the United States.
• There is a lack of accepted safety for use of the drug or other substance under medical supervision.
• Some Schedule I substances are ecstasy, heroin, LSD, and marijuana.

Schedule II

• The drug or other substance has a high potential for abuse.
• The drug or other substance has a currently accepted medical use in treatment in the United States or a currently accepted medical use with severe restrictions.
• Abuse of the drug or other substance may lead to severe psychological or physical dependence.
• Schedule II substances include morphine, PCP, cocaine, methadone, and methamphetamine.

Schedule III

• The drug or other substance has a potential for abuse less than the drugs or other substances in Schedules I and II.
• The drug or other substance has a currently accepted medical use in treatment in the United States.
• Abuse of the drug or other substance may lead to moderate or low physical dependence or high psychological dependence.
• Anabolic steroids, codeine, hydrocodone with aspirin or Tylenol, and some barbiturates are Schedule III substances.

Schedule IV

• The drug or other substance has a low potential for abuse relative to the drugs or other substances in Schedule III.
• The drug or other substance has a currently accepted medical use in treatment in the United States.
• Abuse of the drug or other substance may lead to limited physical dependence or psychological dependence relative to the drugs or other substances in Schedule III.
• Included in Schedule IV are Darvon, Talwin, Equanil, Valium, and Xanax.

• The drug or other substance has a low potential for abuse relative to the drugs or other substances in Schedule IV.
• The drug or other substance has a currently accepted medical use in treatment in the United States.
(Source: www.dea.gov)

Ecstasy Timeline: Part One

1912	Merck files for a patent on MDMA.
1927	Dr. Max Oberlin, a Merck chemist, tests MDMA, noting that the chemical is similar to adrenaline.
1953-1954	The U.S. Army conducts secret animal experiments with MDMA and other psychoactive drugs.
1959	Another Merck chemist, Dr. Wolfgang Fruhstorfer, researches MDMA's potential use as a stimulant.
1965	Alexander Shulgin synthesizes MDMA while working at Dow Chemical, but does not try the substance.
1967	Shulgin tries MDMA himself.
1972	Police see MDMA pills on the streets in Chicago. Illicit use begins to spread.
1977	A friend of Shulgin's, psychologist Leo Zeff, begins using MDMA in his practice to help patients overcome emotional barriers.
1984	Michael Clegg names the drug ecstasy, and begins openly selling it in Texas, using advertising, a 1-800 number to place orders, and even offering shipping. At its peak, he was delivering half a million pills a month to the Dallas area.
1985	The Drug Enforcement Administration decides to emergency Schedule MDMA, placing it into Schedule 1.

3 The Effects of Ecstasy

For the first time in my life, I knew what empathy felt like. I thought that everyone was my friend, simply due to the fact that those around me (even if I didn't know them) shared and enhanced this feeling just by being around me. The world seemed like a better place. There was no war, no poverty, no pain while I was rolling. I have never felt closer to my friends who were there until then also. We were sharing something that we all knew the others were feeling. We were all in tune with each other's thoughts, feeling, emotions.

I've given up pilling now, because last week I had to have an abortion—had I not been eeeeing off my face the whole time, I firstly would never have slept with the guy I slept with, let alone done it without contraception! Now the

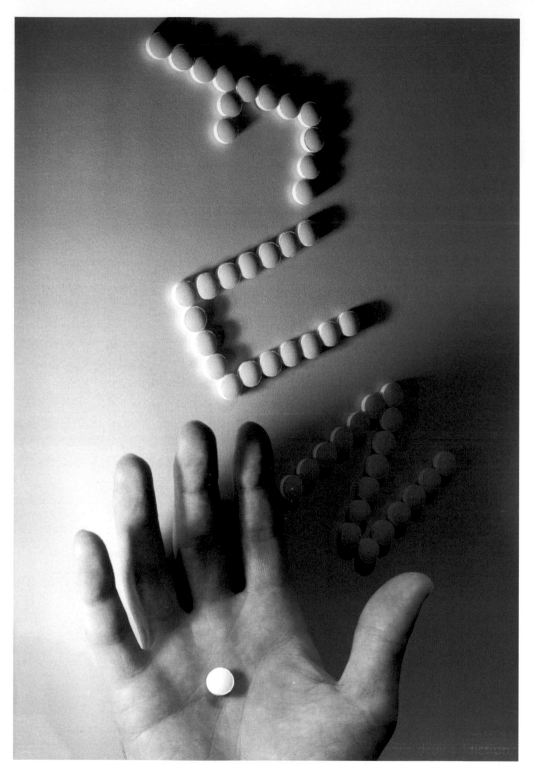

People often begin taking ecstasy simply as a way to have more fun.

Chapter 3—The Effects of Ecstasy

thought of E makes me nauseous and sad—when I first took it, it was the best, best, best thing I'd ever experienced. I remember begging friends to take E with me, and telling them it's different to normal drugs. I don't think it is anymore. It's just such a pity that people can't feel like they do on E naturally.

During the week I would feel depressed and very wound up. I wasn't sleeping properly and was having anxiety attacks. I found the only way to try to keep myself occupied in the weekday evenings and to aid sleep, was to go drinking. A bad move, a year later I was put on antidepressants (Prozac) and my blood pressure was high (dangerously so when having taken E even up to 4 days before), I was suffering pains around the kidney area, and my memory was a complete mess. . . . From my experiences, I would say that . . . the prolonged exposure to chemical happiness can affect considerably the user's ability to be happy for real.

These three stories from the pro-ecstasy website www.ecstasy.org describe different effects of ecstasy. The first person describes a pleasant experience, during which it seemed as though nothing bad could happen ever again. This person felt that he had become closer to his friends, and more in tune with the feelings of others. The girl sharing the second story also enjoyed her experiences taking ecstasy, but her choices while high led her to a very negative situation. The third person is describing a dependence on ecstasy that has begun wearing on him mentally, physically, and emo-

Fast Fact

It takes about fifteen minutes for ecstasy to reach the brain if taken on an empty stomach.

tionally. And these are just three of hundreds of ecstasy experiences described by users online. As with these three, the stories vary from very positive to very negative. How does ecstasy cause this range of responses?

Ecstasy and the Brain

It is no surprise that the major effects of ecstasy are the result of its activity in the brain. After all, the brain is the control center for all the body's physical, emotional and mental capacities.

Before it can begin altering the brain, however, ecstasy must get there. When an ecstasy pill is swallowed, it dissolves quickly in the stomach. Once dissolved in the stomach some ecstasy is absorbed directly into the bloodstream, but most of the MDMA molecules travel from the stomach into the small intestine. From the small intestine, the drug is absorbed into the bloodstream very easily.

Ecstasy molecules travel through the bloodstream from the stomach and small intestines to the liver. The liver *metabolizes* some of the ecstasy while the rest is carried to the heart. From there, the ecstasy is pumped through the lungs along with the blood. The now oxygenated blood travels back to the heart and then carries the ecstasy to the brain and to other organs in body. Normally the *blood-brain barrier* keeps drugs from entering the brain. However, ecstasy is able to cross this barrier and enter into the brain.

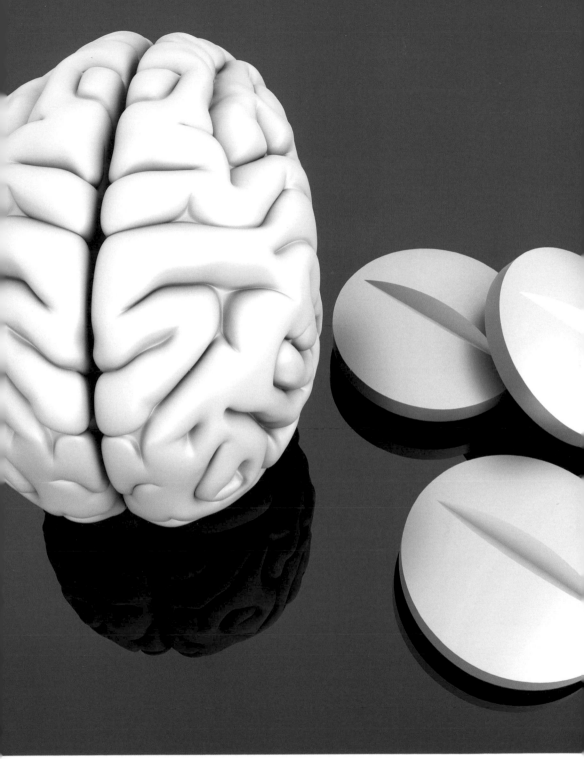

The chemicals within ecstasy alter the way your brain cells function.

Other Neurotransmitters and Their Roles in the Body

Acetylcholine

A neurotransmitter used by spinal cord neurons to control muscles and by many neurons in the brain to regulate memory.

Dopamine

Dopamine produces feelings of pleasure when released by the brain. Dopamine has multiple functions depending on where in the brain it acts.

GABA (gamma-aminobutyric acid)

GABA is the major inhibitory neurotransmitter in the brain.

Glutamate

Glutamate is the most common excitatory neurotransmitter in the brain.

Glycine

A neurotransmitter used mainly by neurons in the spinal cord. It probably always acts as an inhibitory neurotransmitter.

Norepinephrine

Norepinephrine (also called noradrenaline) acts as a neurotransmitter and a hormone. In the peripheral nervous system, it is part of the fight-or-flight response. In the brain, it acts as a neurotransmitter regulating normal brain processes.

Once in the brain, MDMA primarily affects the neurotransmitter serotonin. Neurotransmitters are chemicals that are used as messengers by neurons. These chemicals are released at the end of one neuron (the presynaptic neuron), travel across a space called

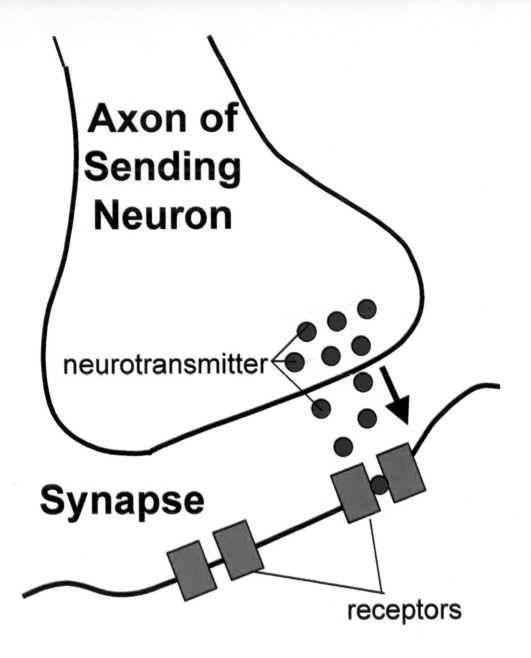

Neurotransmitters bridge the gap between nerve cells, as diagrammed here. By doing this, they influence our moods.

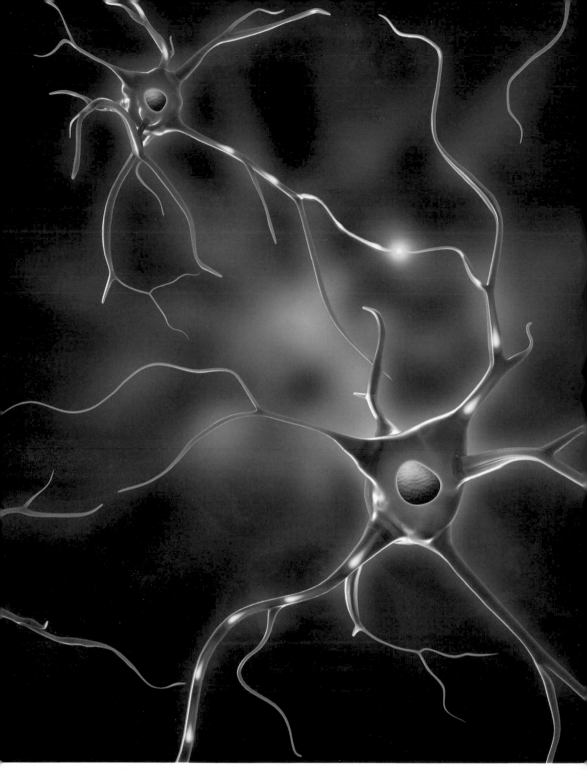

Ecstasy's effects begin at this level, in the spaces between your nerve cells.

the synaptic gap, and are then accepted into receptors on the postsynaptic neuron. Neurotransmitters are usually excitatory, meaning they trigger an action in the receiving cell, but they can also be inhibitory, when they block an action. Serotonin is usually inhibitory, and it plays an important role in regulating mood, aggression, sexual activity, sleep, and sensitivity to pain. In the spinal cord, serotonin is inhibitory in pain pathways. In other words, serotonin helps to reduce feelings of pain. Low serotonin levels result in increased sensitivity to pain. Serotonin also constricts blood vessels, and helps the body regulate its temperature.

The MDMA molecule attaches itself to the serotonin transporter, which takes serotonin out of the gap between neurons, thus ending the "communication" between the neurons. MDMA is able to attach itself to the serotonin transporter because its chemical structure is similar to that of serotonin. When MDMA binds to this transporter, the serotonin stays in the gap longer, and thus prolongs the serotonin signal. MDMA also makes neurons produce extra serotonin. MDMA has similar effects on the neurotransmitters norepinephrine and dopamine.

Effects of Ecstasy

MDMA's affect on brain chemistry leads to the psychological and physical effects of the drug. Some of these effects are positive (what users hope for) and some of the effects are negative. For example, the extra serotonin in the brain causes the positive effect on mood that people experience while on ecstasy as well as the undesirable and dangerous effect of *hyperthermia*. The effects of ecstasy, whether positive or negative, can generally be expected to last about three to six hours.

The increased amount of norepinephrine can cause increases in heart rate and blood pressure. MDMA also causes an increase in the amount of dopamine in the body, which adds to its stimulant effects and may result in the desire to take more ecstasy. Dopamine is part of the brain's reward system, which seeks more of something that gives pleasure. Drugs that are addictive all cause changes within the brain's reward pathway.

Other short-term adverse effects of ecstasy include confusion, impaired thinking, agitation, and disturbed behavior. Negative physical effects include excessive sweating, dry mouth, increased heart rate, fatigue, muscle spasms (especially jaw clenching), and as mentioned earlier, increased body temperature. These problems can occur from soon after taking the drug to days or weeks after use.

Long-term use of ecstasy can cause depression, sleep problems, drug craving, and severe anxiety. In addition, chronic users of ecstasy often perform more poorly than nonusers on tests of brain function and memory. Many of these effects occur because the body's normal serotonin production may be altered by the repeated use of ecstasy. Research in animals indicates that MDMA can be neurotoxic, or harmful to the brain; one study in nonhuman primates showed that exposure to MDMA for only four days caused damage that was still evident six to seven years later. Although the same results have not been replicated in human studies, the animal research strongly suggests that MDMA is not a safe drug for humans.

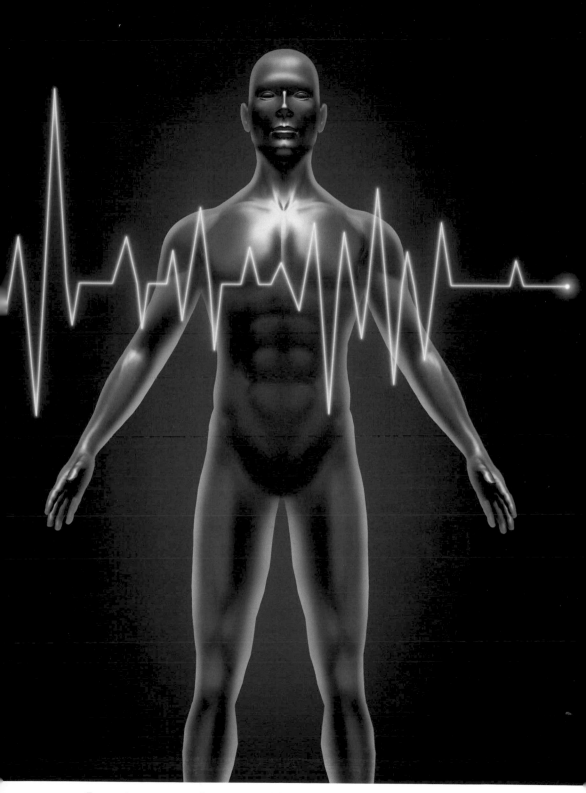

Ecstasy increases your heart rate and blood pressure. Eventually, this can become dangerous.

x

Ecstasy—Dangerous Euphoria 51

What Do You Know About Ecstasy?

1. The scientific term for Ecstasy is _____.
A. MDMA
B. PCP
C. LSD

2. MDMA is known as a "club drug" because _____.
A. teens take MDMA at a clubhouse
B. teens take MDMA in a big sandwich
C. some teens use MDMA at all-night dance clubs

3. MDMA has _____.
A. part opiate and part inhalant properties
B. part stimulant and part hallucinogenic properties
C. part marijuana and part prescription drug properties

4. One of the slang words for MDMA is _____.
A. dumbo
B. Adam
C. noodles

5. MDMA is usually taken in a _____.
A. needle or syringe
B. patch on the skin
C. pill, tablet, or capsule

6. One of the dangers of MDMA abuse is hyperthermia, which means _____.
A. extreme overheating
B. freezing
C. losing an arm or a leg

7. MDMA is _____ in animals.
A. neurotoxic
B. hypertoxic
C. not toxic

8. MDMA use can affect _____.
A. sight and hearing
B. thought and memory

C. speech and language

9. A tablet of MDMA often includes _____.
A. other chemicals or substances
B. added vitamins
C. artificial sweetener

10. A "hit" of MDMA can last _____.
A. all night
B. 30 minutes
C. 3 to 6 hours

This quiz was produced by the National Institute on Drug Abuse, National Institutes of Health, U.S. Department of Health and Human Services (teens.drugabuse.gov).

Answers

1. A. The scientific term for Ecstasy is MDMA (3,4-methylenedioxymethamphetamine).
2. C. MDMA is known as a "club drug" because teens and young adults have taken the drug at a nightclub or all-night party.
3. B. MDMA is part stimulant (amphetamine-like) and part hallucinogen (LSD-like).
4. B. MDMA is sometimes called "Adam."
5. C. MDMA is usually taken by mouth, as a pill, tablet, or capsule.
6. A. One of the dangers of MDMA abuse is hyperthermia—extreme overheating— because of dehydration or loss of fluids through excessive sweating.
7. A. MDMA is neurotoxic in animals, which means it can damage the brain.
8. B. MDMA use can affect thought and memory.
9. A. Other chemicals or substances are often added to or substituted for MDMA, such as caffeine, dextromethorphan (cough syrup), and amphetamine. Makers of MDMA can add anything they want to the drug, so its purity is always questionable.
10. C. For most MDMA users, a "hit" can last 3 to 6 hours.

Dangerous Effects

Ecstasy's effects can become worse if the person is exercising while taking it—which is exactly what people do at raves. In severe cases, people have died from seizures and strokes, as well as cardiovascular and kidney failure.

DSM-IV-TR Criteria for Dependence

• continued use despite knowledge of physical or psychological harm
• withdrawal effects
• tolerance

As a result of the drug's increased use, the amount of ecstasy-related emergency-room cases increased by four times between 1998 and 2000 alone. The amount of deaths involving ecstasy has also increased. "One of the biggest problems we're having with ecstasy is people thinking if you die from it, you're not using it right," said Brian Blake, spokesman for the White House Office of National Drug Control Policy. The reality is—there is no safe "right" way to use the drug.

Long-term Consequences

Many of ecstasy's dangers may occur in ways that scientists are just beginning to understand. Even first-time users have shown after-effects such as depression, anxiety, aggressiveness, paranoia, and sleep disorders. They may become immediately psychologically and physically addicted to the drug. According to the National Institute on Drug Abuse (NIDA), a study on monkeys showed that exposure to MDMA (ecstasy) twice a day for four straight days caused brain damage—and that damage was

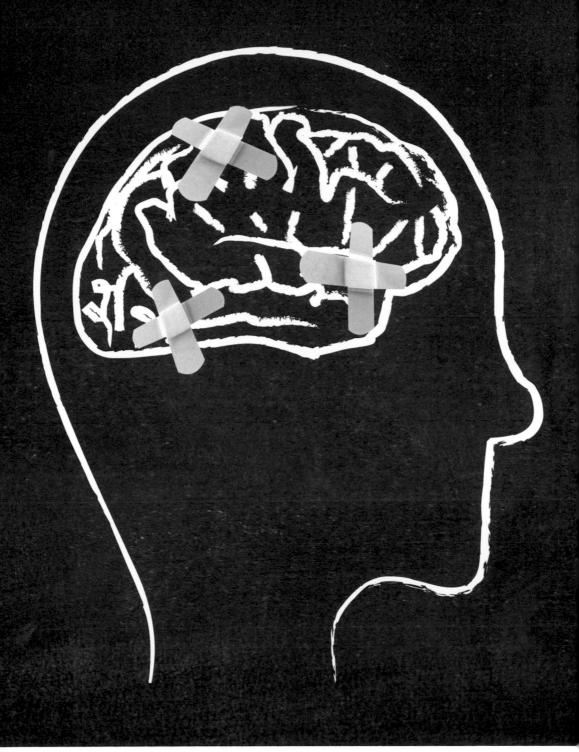

Your brain is probably the most important tool you have for dealing with life successfully, so you need to take care of it. It is amazingly resilient—but once damaged, it is also very difficult to repair.

This is pure MDMA crystal. People who take ecstasy at a party, however, have no way of knowing if this is what they're getting—or if the pills they consume also contain other substances as well.

still there six to seven years later. Humans who take ecstasy, particularly adolescents, whose brains are still developing, may also be risking permanent brain damage.

Mixing MDMA with other chemicals poses another risk to the user. Many ecstasy users take the drug in combination with other substances, commonly alcohol or marijuana. Again, the body's ability to metabolize each drug is reduced as more chemicals are taken into the body. In addition, other drugs that are chemically similar to MDMA, such as MDA and PMA, are sometimes sold as ecstasy. These drugs pose additional health risks to the user. PMA sold as ecstasy has been linked to deaths in the United States and Australia. Finally, ecstasy tablets are often laced with other substances, such as ephedrine (a stimulant); dextromethorphan (DXM, a cough suppressant); ketamine (an anesthetic used mostly by veterinarians); caffeine; cocaine; or methamphetamine.

Is Ecstasy Addictive?

This is a question that scientists and health professionals are still working to answer. For some people, it seems that ecstasy can be addictive. A 2001 study of young adult and adolescent MDMA users found that 43 percent of those who reported ecstasy use met the accepted DSM-IV-TR criteria for dependence. Also, in a research setting, monkeys will choose to give ecstasy to themselves (by pressing a lever to get an injection). Studies have found that monkeys do not choose to give themselves drugs that are not addictive. In addition, research shows that ecstasy works in a specific pathway within the brain called the "reward pathway,"

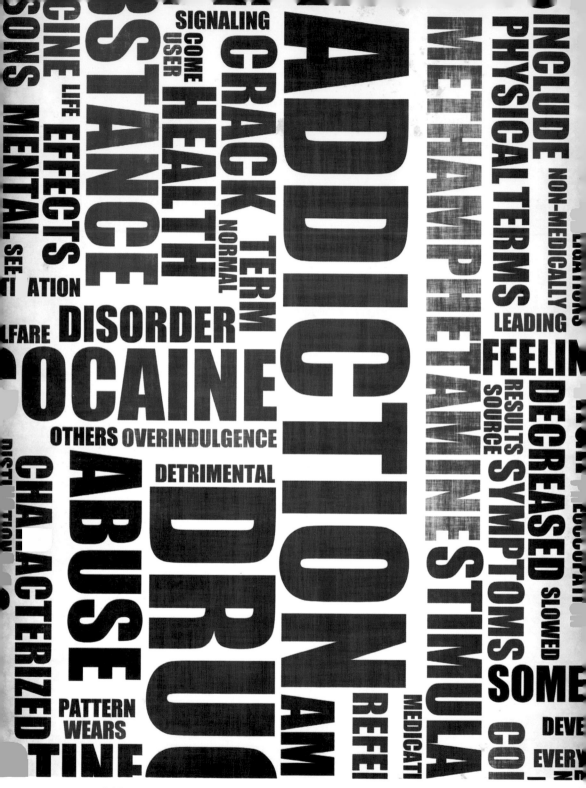

Addiction is a complicated topic. People don't always agree even on what the word means. But clearly, it's a major problem in our world today.

which can explain why a person wants to do it again and again. All addictive drugs act in some way within the reward pathway.

Whether ecstasy is addictive or not is just one of the *controversial* issues surrounding the drug. Since it was first made illegal, certain groups of people have been calling for a reevaluation of its benefits as a therapeutic drug.

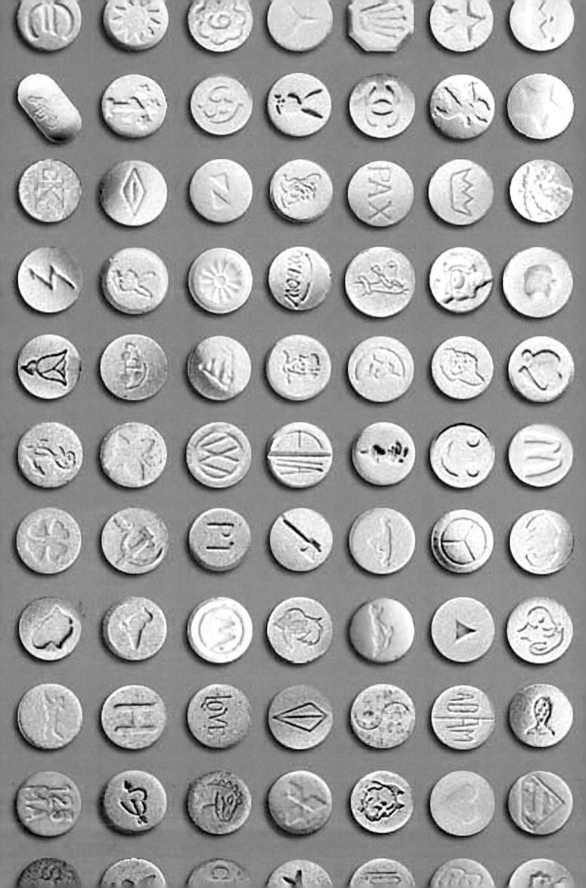

4 Controversial Issues

Ecstasy has helped me to live with schizophrenia. You see the medication that is currently given for schizophrenia helps to limit the symptoms (and it does so in some cases more than others), but you are left on your own to deal with whatever symptoms that may remain. Ecstasy helps to bridge that gap, it helps you to live with whatever symptoms you may have that the medication doesn't help with. I still live with **paranoid** symptoms everyday, but I am now okay with that. I accept myself for who I am, I can live with being schizophrenic. It was ecstasy that helped me come to these terms.

I came to this realization with just myself and ecstasy, I had no therapist to guide me in this area. I've had lots of therapy, but none of it really compares to what ecstasy and myself have taught me.

One can only imagine how much better ecstasy therapy would be for me if I had an experienced therapist to guide me.

I continue to use ecstasy, and I will continue to use it in limited amounts until something better, or a cure for schizophrenia comes along. I do want to make it clear that ecstasy is in no way a substitution for the proper medication in dealing with schizophrenia. Medication remains essential in keeping this disease in check. Ecstasy is simply another kind of medication that should be used (infrequently) to supplement the more traditional medications.

The individual who posted the story anonymously at www.ecstasy.org has been struggling with schizophrenia his whole life. After years of unsuccessful treatments, this individual claims to have had a breakthrough because of ecstasy. However, since ecstasy is an illegal drug, the "treatment" can only be self-administered. He wonders how much better he could get with a professional prescribing the ecstasy and guiding him through therapy sessions.

This person is not the only person calling for a reevaluation of ecstasy's illegal status. To some extent there is a debate regarding the illegal status of all illicit drugs, but the debate about ecstasy is different. From the moment ecstasy was first declared a Schedule I drug there have been people arguing that it has medicinal properties and needs to be reclassified as Schedule II or III.

Some people believe that doctors should be able to legally administer ecstasy as a legitimate treatment for psychological disorders.

The DEA's Top Ten Facts on Legalization

Fact 1: We have made significant progress in fighting drug use and drug trafficking in America. Now is not the time to abandon our efforts.

The Legalization Lobby claims that the fight against drugs cannot be won. However, overall drug use is down by more than a third in the last twenty years, while cocaine use has dropped by an astounding 70 percent. Ninety-five percent of Americans do not use drugs. This is success by any standards.

Fact 2: A balanced approach of prevention, enforcement, and treatment is the key in the fight against drugs.

A successful drug policy must apply a balanced approach of prevention, enforcement and treatment. All three aspects are crucial. For those who end up hooked on drugs, there are innovative programs, like Drug Treatment Courts, that offer non-violent users the option of seeking treatment. Drug Treatment Courts provide court supervision, unlike voluntary treatment centers.

Fact 3: Illegal drugs are illegal because they are harmful.

There is a growing misconception that some illegal drugs can be taken safely. For example, savvy drug dealers have learned how to market drugs like Ecstasy to youth. Some in the Legalization Lobby even claim such drugs have medical value, despite the lack of conclusive scientific evidence.

Fact 4: Smoked marijuana is not scientifically approved medicine. Marinol, the legal version of medical marijuana, is approved by science.

According to the Institute of Medicine, there is no future in smoked marijuana as medicine. However, the prescription drug Marinol—a legal and safe version of medical marijuana which isolates the active ingredient of THC—has been studied and approved by the Food & Drug Administration as safe medicine. The difference is that you have to get a prescription for Marinol from a licensed physician. You can't buy it on a street corner, and you don't smoke it.

Fact 5: Drug control spending is a minor portion of the U.S. budget. Compared to the social costs of drug abuse and addiction, government spending on drug control is minimal.

The Legalization Lobby claims that the United States has wasted billions of dollars in its anti-drug efforts. But for those kids saved from drug addiction, this is hardly wasted dollars. Moreover, our fight against drug abuse and addiction is an ongoing struggle that should be treated like any other social problem. Would we give up on education or poverty simply because we haven't eliminated all problems? Compared to the social costs of drug abuse and addiction—whether in taxpayer dollars or in pain and suffering—government spending on drug control is minimal.

Fact 6: Legalization of drugs will lead to increased use and increased levels of addiction.
Legalization has been tried before—and failed miserably. Alaska's experiment with Legalization in the 1970s led to the state's teens using marijuana at more than twice the rate of other youths nationally. This led Alaska's residents to vote to re-criminalize marijuana in 1990.

Fact 7: Crime, violence, and drug use go hand-in-hand.
Crime, violence and drug use go hand in hand. Six times as many homicides are committed by people under the influence of drugs, as by those who are looking for money to buy drugs. Most drug crimes aren't committed by people trying to pay for drugs; they're committed by people on drugs.

Fact 8: Alcohol has caused significant health, social, and crime problems in this country, and legalized drugs would only make the situation worse.
The Legalization Lobby claims drugs are no more dangerous than alcohol. But drunk driving is one of the primary killers of Americans. Do we want our bus drivers, nurses, and airline pilots to be able to take drugs one evening, and operate freely at work the next day? Do we want to add to the destruction by making drugged driving another primary killer?

Fact 9: Europe's more liberal drug policies are not the right model for America.
The Legalization Lobby claims that the "European Model" of the drug problem is successful. However, since legalization of marijuana in Holland, heroin addiction levels have tripled. And Needle Park seems like a poor model for America.

Fact 10: Most non-violent drug users get treatment, not jail time.
The Legalization Lobby claims that America's prisons are filling up with users. Truth is, only about 5 percent of inmates in federal prison are there because of simple possession. Most drug criminals are in jail—even on possession charges—because they have plea-bargained down from major trafficking offences or more violent drug crimes.

(Source: www.justice.gov/dea/demand/speakout/index.html)

President Reagan's wife Nancy played an important role in the War on Drugs with her "Just Say No" campaign.

The Legalization Debate in General

Ever since the **War on Drugs** took off in the 1970s, Americans have argued about whether it helped or hurt the country. Even people who believe drugs are harmful don't all agree with the actions taken by the War on Drugs.

Dr. Benson Roe, a retired heart surgeon who campaigns for the legalization of drugs, believes that making drugs legal would allow the FDA (Food and Drug Administration) to oversee the production and sale of these drugs. This would mean the FDA could make sure the drugs were not contaminated. If recreational drugs were legal, Roe argues, billions of dollars would be saved that is now being used on drug prevention, law enforcement, and keeping people in prison for drug-related crimes. Since most gangs earn their money through trafficking in illegal drugs and many homicides are drug-related, these problems would be greatly reduced by legalizing drugs.

In direct reaction to arguments like the ones made by Dr. Roe, the DEA put together a booklet called *Speaking Out Against Drug Legalization*. The booklet gives information that is meant to respond directly to the information presented by proponents of legalization. Point-by-point, the booklet gives the facts on legalization and describes what might happen if the U.S. drug policy were changed.

The Ecstasy Debate

The debate about the status of ecstasy differs from the general legalization debate in that most proponents of medical ecstasy are not trying to legalize it as a street drug. Rather, the pro-ecstasy group wants ecstasy to be available for use by therapists and psychiatrists as a treatment for patients.

In its earliest years, while ecstasy was gaining popularity as a club drug, it was also earning a reputation among psychiatrists as a valuable tool during therapy sessions. Indeed, Alexander Shulgin, who created and tested hundreds of psychoactive drugs, called MDMA the drug with the most promise for use in psychotherapy.

In 1977, Shulgin shared some MDMA with his psychologist friend Leo Zeff, who began treating some of his patients with MDMA. Zeff introduced other therapists to MDMA, and by the mid-1980s, MDMA had gained a reputation as a wonder drug, which allowed patients to get to the heart of their problems much faster than they would have without the drug.

George Greer, a psychiatrist who from 1980 to 1985 conducted over a hundred therapy sessions using MDMA (when it was still legal), states, "Without exception, every therapist who I talked to or even heard of, every therapist who gave MDMA to a patient, was highly impressed by the results." Greer published numerous articles about the therapeutic value of MDMA. In one he explains that MDMA was so effective because it "reduced defensiveness and fear of emotional injury, thereby facilitating more direct expression of feelings and opinions, and enabling people to receive both praise and criticism with more acceptance than usual."

However, all such reports about the benefits of MDMA in therapy were anecdotal, meaning they were not based on regulated *clinical* testing, but just on stories from its use in the real world. Anecdotal evidence

Leo Zeff believed that MDMA was a powerful therapeutic drug in the treatment of psychological issues.

Drug Approval

Before a drug can be marketed in the United States, it must be officially approved by the Food and Drug Administration (FDA). Today's FDA is the primary consumer protection agency in the United States. Operating under the authority given it by the government, and guided by laws established throughout the twentieth century, the FDA has established a rigorous drug approval process that verifies the safety, effectiveness, and accuracy of labeling for any drug marketed in the United States.

While the United States has the FDA for the approval and regulation of drugs and medical devices, Canada has a similar organization called the Therapeutic Product Directorate (TPD). The TPD is a division of Health Canada, the Canadian government's department of health. The TPD regulates drugs, medical devices, disinfectants, and sanitizers with disinfectant claims. Some of the things that the TPD monitors are quality, effectiveness, and safety. Just as the FDA must approve new drugs in the United States, the TPD must approve new drugs in Canada before those drugs can enter the market.

is not strong enough to prove the safety or usefulness of a drug. Drugs that will be sold and used in the United States must go through many levels of testing before they can be approved by the Food and Drug Administration (FDA). Once a drug is labeled as a Schedule I drug, approval must be obtained from both the FDA and the DEA before scientists are even allowed to do research on the drug. This is why therapists in 1985 fought so hard against MDMA being classified as a Schedule I drug.

The other side of the debate is the DEA, which describes ecstasy as a dangerous, potentially addictive drug with no known medicinal value. While studies have shown that ecstasy causes brain damage, and it is addictive for some users, the assertion that it has no medicinal value is being challenged.

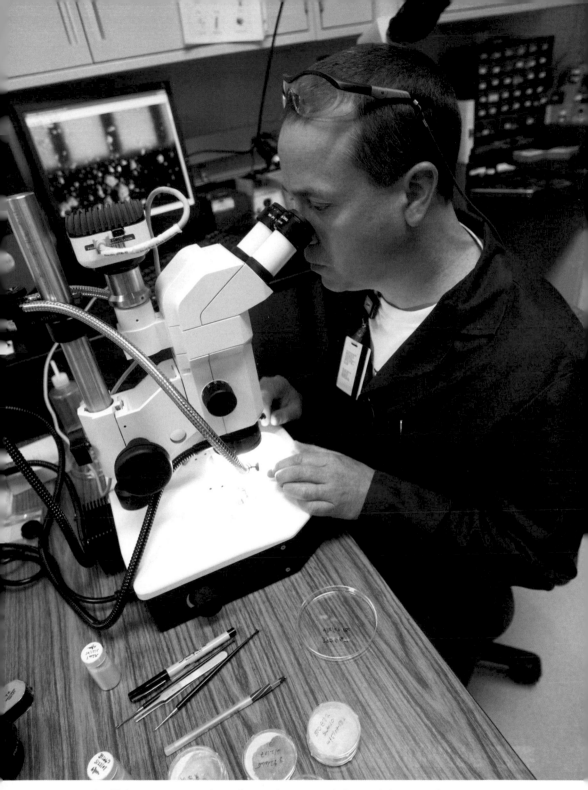

An FDA scientist at work, analyzing the potential chemical dangers of various substances.

The FDA is one of the U.S. government's watchdog agencies, protecting the safety of the American public in many ways.

Harvard's Psychedelic History

The MDMA research that started in 2008 at Harvard's McLean Hospital is not the first psychedelic experiment to be conducted at the institution.

In the summer of 1960, Timothy Leary, a psychology lecturer at Harvard University, traveled to Mexico to try hallucinogenic psilocybin mushrooms. He returned to Harvard feeling as though his life had been changed by his experience, that he now saw the world differently, and that the drug had helped him discover "the god within." With a colleague, Richard Alpert, Leary began the Harvard Psychedelic Drug Research Program, a series of experiments studying the effects of psilocybin and other hallucinogens on people. One example of the project's work was the Concord Prison Experiment, a study on whether psilocybin could help keep prisoners from going back to a criminal lifestyle once they had been released. Leary believed the results of the experiment were promising, although in the long term the prisoners involved in the study reoffended at about the same rate as those who had never been given psilocybin.

In 1963, Leary and Alpert were both fired from Harvard, after university officials discovered they were giving LSD to undergraduate students. Leary moved to an estate outside New York City and continued his research on psychedelic drugs. He also continued arguing for the usefulness of psychedelics in helping people expand their consciousness. People curious about LSD and other hallucinogens came from all over to meet Leary and to take drugs with him. At this point, most hallucinogens were still legal in the United States.

Clinical Trials

In 2000 the FDA approved the first clinical trial studying the use of MDMA during therapy for patients suffering from *post-traumatic stress disorder* (PTSD). Dr. Michael Mithoefer of Charleston, South Carolina, is the lead researcher for the study, sponsored by the Multidisciplinary Association for Psychedelic Studies (MAPS). An article published in the *Journal of Psy-*

chopharmacology in July 2010 suggests that the results are promising. Twenty patients suffering from chronic PTSD were treated with a combination of psychotherapy and MDMA. The study found that after treatment over 80 percent of participants no longer met the criteria for PTSD, compared to only 25 percent of the *placebo* group.

The treatment seems to be successful because the MDMA allows patients to relive their traumatic experience without experiencing the fear or stress that normally accompanies the memory. While on MDMA, the patients feel an increase in their ability to communicate with and trust other people (empathy). Therefore, the drug allows the patients to be more open with the therapist, thus making the psychotherapy more effective.

The study is still ongoing, and researchers need to investigate long-term effects before the study can be considered a success. However, the preliminary results are good enough to allow the FDA to approve further studies, with more participants. In addition, the FDA has approved a Harvard-based study of the effects of MDMA-assisted psychotherapy for advanced-stage cancer patients struggling with anxiety. Tests began in February of 2008.

In a sense, the debate is similar to the debate about the legalization of medical marijuana. However, the active chemical of marijuana (THC) can be extracted and made into medicine that can be taken in pill form. The pills should therefore have the desired medical effects without some of the other effects of marijuana (which contains hundreds of other chemicals). MDMA is what it is—there are no other chemicals involved.

Ecstasy Timeline: Part Two

1984	Psychiatrists, therapists, and other scientists and doctors who had been using MDMA in their practices challenge the DEA Scheduling, resulting in government hearings on how MDMA should be scheduled.
1986	The judge in the hearings decides that MDMA should not be placed higher than Schedule III.
1986	The DEA declares MDMA permanently Schedule I.
1988	After years of debate and trials, courts agree with Justice Young's original opinion and order the DEA to reassess the Scheduling of ecstasy.
1988	The DEA again decides that MDMA is a Schedule I drug.
March 2001	The U.S. government increases penalties for use and distribution of ecstasy.
November 2001	The U.S. Food and Drug Administration (FDA) gives approval for human testing of MDMA for the treatment of post-traumatic stress disorder (PTSD) to the Multidisciplinary Association for Psychedelic Studies (MAPS).
September 2003	Con-MDMA researcher George Ricaurte confesses that one of his most recent studies proving the dangers of MDMA was falsified.
September 2003	MAPS is granted Institutional Review Board (IRB) approval for human research with MDMA.
April 2004	The first dose of MDMA in MAPS' post-traumatic stress disorder study is administered.
2007	Harvard study testing the use of MDMA to relieve anxiety and pain in terminal cancer patients begins.
2010	Start of MAPS-sponsored study into using MDMA to treat veterans with PTSD.

FDA scientists analyze many kinds of chemical data in order to determine the
safety of various drugs and food products.

Even though therapy doses of MDMA will be lower, and carefully administered by medical professionals, a person taking the drug for therapy will still have the same response as a person taking it at a club, meaning it could have the same negative side effects. Proponents of therapeutic ecstasy argue that all legally prescribed drugs have potential side effects—the question that must be answered is, "Do the benefits outweigh the risks?" Studies like the PTSD study in South Carolina and the cancer patient study at Harvard hope to prove that they do.

5 Legal Consequences

Ever since the late 1960s, when President Richard Nixon declared a "war on drugs," the legal consequences for using drugs, selling them, or manufacturing or growing them have been harsh. With the increased popularity and availability of drugs during the 1960s, the entire world began to realize how dangerous they were.

In 1970, the United States passed the Controlled Substances Act. The Act divided drugs into groups, called schedules. Schedule I drugs have the most restrictions and the strictest penalties associated with them. They are described as drugs with no accepted medical uses and a high risk for abuse.

President Richard Nixon put into motion the policies that set America on the road to considering drug use as a crime to be fought through the legal system.

Drug Laws in the United States

The laws about illegal drugs can be very complicated. There are federal laws and state laws, and which law enforcement agency has *jurisdiction* depends on a number of factors. The United States Drug Enforcement Administration (DEA) is the federal law enforcement agency with jurisdiction over federal offenses. Among other things, a federal crime occurs whenever someone takes illegal drugs across a state line or takes them onto federal land.

While the Controlled Substances Act is the set of laws governing federal drug offenses, each state also has its own set of drug laws. In some states, possession of small amounts of certain drugs are classified as misdemeanors, lesser offenses that are generally punished with fines, *probation*, community service, or light prison sentences. Other states have tougher laws and almost all drug-related charges are felonies. Felonies have harsher penalties than misdemeanors, and people also view these crimes much more seriously. People with felony convictions on their records can find it difficult to find jobs, rent apartments, or be accepted to college (especially law school). They usually cannot own a gun or run for public office, and a few states permanently ban those who have been convicted of a felony from ever voting again.

Crimes Related to Drugs

The most basic drug-related crime is possession. This means a person has an illegal drug with him, whether or not he intends to use the drug himself, sell it, or give it to a friend. If a person has a large amount of drugs

Ecstasy withdrawal symptoms include but are not limited to:

- anxiety
- panic attacks
- inability to sleep
- depression
- psychosis
- irritability
- paranoia
- intense craving for the drug
- loss of appetite

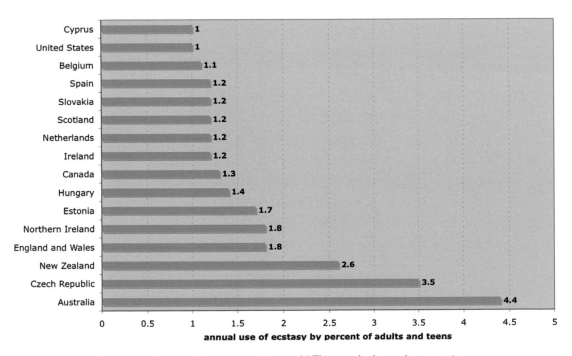

Country	annual use of ecstasy by percent of adults and teens
Cyprus	1
United States	1
Belgium	1.1
Spain	1.2
Slovakia	1.2
Scotland	1.2
Netherlands	1.2
Ireland	1.2
Canada	1.3
Hungary	1.4
Estonia	1.7
Northern Ireland	1.8
England and Wales	1.8
New Zealand	2.6
Czech Republic	3.5
Australia	4.4

Ecstasy use is a problem around the world. This graph shows the countries where ecstasy use is most common. (Source: UN World Drug Report, 2008)

with him, he may be charged with possession with intent to distribute, a more serious offense; laws usually declare that anything over a certain amount—an amount which varies from drug to drug, as well as from state to state—is more than anyone would reasonably have for personal use. For example, in New York State, possession of a single ecstasy pill is considered a misdemeanor, which could result in up to a year in jail. Possession of more than five grams is considered a Class B felony, and carries a jail sentence between one and nine years.

Selling or distributing drugs is sometimes called drug trafficking. This can mean dealing in drugs on a very large scale, such as drug cartels that smuggle drugs across international borders, or it can mean smaller operations involving only a single dealer. The first offense for trafficking any amount of ecstasy is a maximum of twenty years and a fine of one million dollars. If there is death or serious injury along with the trafficking charge, then twenty years is the minimum sentence. Even if the amount of the drug is very small, a person can still be charged with trafficking if a police officer sees her give some to another person. Therefore, someone does not even need to sell drugs to be charged with trafficking—giving the drugs to a friend to hold for a moment would still be looked at as trafficking.

Another crime often associated with drugs is conspiracy. Conspiracy means that two or more people have agreed together to commit a crime. Someone can be charged with conspiracy if, for example, she lends her car to her brother who then uses the car to pick up a shipment of illegal drugs. Being friends with people who use

Drug Laws in Canada

In Canada, the Controlled Drugs and Substances Act (CDSA) contains the laws concerning illegal drugs. Like the U.S. Controlled Substances Act, the CDSA also puts restricted drugs into schedules, although the Canadian and American drug schedules do not correspond with each other. The CDSA lays out eight drug schedules, and the schedule a person is charged under determines the maximum sentence she can receive. The strictest penalties are for offensives related to Schedule I drugs. The maximum penalty for possession of a Schedule I drug is seven years in prison, and the maximum penalty for trafficking or producing a Schedule I drug is a life sentence.

and distribute drugs can be very dangerous, since otherwise innocent actions could result in an arrest on conspiracy charges.

Sometimes, while using or distributing drugs, a person commits another crime. For example, a drug dealer may kill a rival. Another example would be a person who breaks into a house or commits a murder while under the influence of drugs, because the drug has lowered his inhibitions or strengthened violent emotions he already had. Hallucinogenic drugs, however, are less likely to influence a person to commit a violent crime than are certain other drugs, such as methamphetamine.

A special case of this type of crime is driving while under the influence of drugs. This is called DUI, or, sometimes DWI (Driving While Impaired) or OWI (Operating While Impaired). The exact term depends on the state where the crime was committed. If someone is injured or killed by a person who has been taking drugs or alcohol while driving, the penalties are much higher.

People caught up in the euphoria of ecstasy are not as likely to commit violent crimes as other drug users might be.

Ecstasy—Dangerous Euphoria 85

DRUG FREE
SCHOOL ZONE
VIOLATORS WILL BE PROSECUTED

SPONSORED BY
COMMUNITY SCHOOL
DISTRICT ONE
YOUTH LEADERSHIP PROGRAM

COURTESY OF CITIBANK

Leo Lawrence	William Ubiñas	Norman Whitlow
Chairperson, CSB	Superintendent	Director, Youth Leadership

Drug Free Zones are intended to create areas where drug dealers will be less likely to take the risk of doing business, thus protecting young people.

Drugs and Teens

Some teens think they are safe when they experiment with drugs. Typically, the penalties for juvenile offenders are much lighter than for adults, and a person can petition the courts to have her record erased after she turns eighteen. Over the past decade, however, many of the laws protecting juvenile offenders have changed. Today, young offenders have less privacy than in the past, and their record can often continue to haunt them throughout their lives.

Bringing drugs onto school grounds can also create huge problems for students. Many schools have very strict policies about drugs on school property, and a student who breaks the rules can be suspended or even expelled. Losing even part of a school year can be difficult to catch up.

Laws in the United States have created Drug Free School Zones around schools, parks, and public housing. The purpose of the zones is to keep drug dealers away from kids and teens. Under the current laws, the zones extend 1,000 feet from school property and 500 feet from parks and public housing. Within the zones, penalties for drug convictions are greater, and the zones are usually patrolled more attentively. In 2006, some lawmakers began asking for smaller zones but with increased penalties for convictions. Many cities have so many Drug Free School Zones that the zones overlap and cover almost the entire city. This means, basically, that the city has simply toughened their drug laws and the original intent of the law—to keep drugs away from kids—is lost.

Legal consequences of using drugs, or of simply holding them for a friend, can be extremely serious. Law en-

Some people believe that a better use of federal money would be classes like this one, which educate children about the dangers of drug use.

forcement agencies have spent billions of dollars working to wipe out illegal drug use—patrolling the streets, and arresting and imprisoning dealers. Some people believe too much money has been spent, and that a better use of this money would be for treatment programs and prevention by educating the public about the dangers of drugs.

6 Treatment & Prevention

I did E for the first time when I was twelve, because my friend's older brother was doing it, and I wanted to be cool and fit in. Once you start (using drugs) you don't stop, and once you get into that crowd that uses drugs you don't want to. You feel like that's where you fit in, and anybody that doesn't do drugs isn't cool enough for you to hang out with.

And you're feeling good, so you'll do whatever makes you happy for the moment. And the next day you sit down, and you think about it, and you're like, "Oh my God . . . I had unprotected sex with this guy," you know. I don't know how many girls he's ever been with, what if I got something? I was in that situation and had to go get HIV tested. You can really do things you wouldn't normally do when you were sober and thinking straight.

This is an excerpt from a story on www.pbs.org/inthemix/shows/show_ecstasy2.html, where real teens talk about their experiences with club drugs, including ecstasy. There may still be a question about whether ecstasy is addictive, but it is clear from these stories that for various reasons it is hard to stop using E once you start.

Another teen on the same site discusses how he never wanted to end up in rehab, and that one of his most difficult moments was realizing that he had to ask for help.

> I was in a group [rehab] session for 24 hours. We weren't allowed to sleep. And I left and I was like wow, I have so much in common with these people. I got these people to help me, and even to this day I love everybody in that group because they got something that I was never able to give before.

Except in extremely rare cases (and television shows and movies), most people who become addicted to a substance do so on their own; no one forces them to take—or keep taking—a drug. This fact leads many with substance abuse problems to believe that they can beat their addiction on their own. Sadly, this generally results in repeated failures at sobriety, at least in the long run.

So, why *can't* individuals stop using ecstasy on their own? If the drug use has only occurred for a short time, they often can. But, the longer an individual has been

Thunderdome 7.8x5.2mm 53mg MDMA	Triangle 10.2x4.1mm 98mg MDEA	Lips 8.1x5.4mm 61mg MDMA	Killers 9.1x4.3mm 136mg MDMA + caffeine	Number One 8.2x4.8mm 56mg MDMA
Star 8.7x5.4mm g amphetamine race caffeine	Clover Leaf 7x6x4.8mm 46mg MDMA + 19mg MDEA	Sunrise 9.1x4.6mm 129mg MDEA	Diamond 12.7x7.3x4.5mm 102mg MDEA	Twins 9.2x4.2mm 79mg MDMA
edes 8.6x5.2mm g amphetamine trace caffeine	Micro 3.8x1.7mm LSD	Dove 9.2x3.0mm 67mg MDMA + 31mg MDEA	Euro 9.2x2.8mm 57mg MDMA	Red Playboy 9.1x3.2 27mg amphetamin + trace caffeine
phin 9.2x3.6mm 26mg MDEA + 5mg MDMA	TNT 10.1x3.4mm 55mg MBDB	Triangle 10.1x4.3mm 107mg MDEA	Pyramid 10.1x4.6mm medicine called Neo-Cibalgin	CD 8.1x4.0mm 9mg amphetamine + trace caffeine
ple 9.2x3.7mm 42mg MDMA trace caffeine	E-mail 4.5x8.5mm 71mg MDMA	One Two Five 9.1x2.6mm 41mg MDMA	Dove 9.1x3.0mm 18mg amphetamine + trace caffeine	Adidas 8.7x9.3mm 8mg amphetamine + trace caffeine

This postcard was issued to warn users of the actual contents of various kinds of ecstasy pills.

Abuse—or Misuse?

Abuse and misuse are two different things; unfortunately, both can lead to addiction.

Misuse
Patients may forget or not understand their prescription's directions. They may start making their own decisions, perhaps upping the dose in hopes of getting better faster.

Abuse
People may use prescription drugs for nonmedical reasons. Prescription drug abusers may obtain such drugs illegally and use them to get high, fight stress, or boost energy.

using ecstasy, the less likely it is that she can permanently abstain from using it without the help of some kind of a treatment program. Researchers studying drugs and addiction have discovered that when drugs are used over a long period, serious changes occur in how the brain functions. Ecstasy affects the naturally existing level of serotonin in the body. As a result, some users have said that they feel long-term use of ecstasy has affected their ability to be happy without the drug. This drives them to keep going back to the drug for that synthetic happiness. Some of these changes can continue long after the person has stopped taking the drug or substance. If the individual has not learned ways to cope with the continuing cravings to use ecstasy, she will probably relapse.

It's not just the drug's long-term effects on the brain that can doom individual attempts at sobriety. For many addicted to drugs, especially a club drug like ecstasy, the entire drug-taking experience is a time to socialize with friends. Some individuals do not have the strength to stand up to their friends, family, or co-workers and be the only one not using. It's not easy to be the only one not doing something. Peer pressure, especially when combined with changes the substance might have caused in the brain, can make abstinence a non-winnable war.

According to Veterans Affairs Canada, someone may have a problem with drugs if they:

• drink alcohol or use drugs in secret
• suffer blackouts
• have headaches or hangovers
• consume quickly and more often.

The problem may be addiction if any of the following can be answered by yes:

• Are you having problems with any part of your life? Physical health? Work? Family? Mental health? Your social or spiritual life?
• Do you know when to stop drinking? Do you often drink too much and become intoxicated? Do you binge drink?
• Do you have withdrawal symptoms such as shakiness, irritability or seizures when you stop drinking or using drugs?
• Are you using illegal drugs or having your drugs prescribed by more than one doctor?
• Has your drug use increased since you first started using them?
• Are you spending more and more time thinking about where the money for your next drinks or drugs will come from?

(Source: www.veterans.gc.ca/clients/sub.cfm?source=health/wellness/9)

Pharmacological Treatment Programs

Treating drug addiction with drugs? It sounds strange, but for some addictions, like opioid addiction, medications are effective, and even necessary, treatment tools. They are used in both inpatient and outpatient settings.

Most treatment programs use a combination of behavioral treatment and pharmacological methods. Individuals are also encouraged to supplement their programs with support groups. In some cases, participation begins while the individual is still an inpatient.

The right treatment program depends on the substance of addiction and characteristics (such as age) of the individual with the addiction. There are, however, characteristics common to most treatment programs. The first step in overcoming any addiction is to admit there *is* a problem, that you are an addict. In some ways, this may be one of the hardest of a series of incredibly hard steps. But it is impossible to finish the journey to sobriety without taking that first step of admitting to being an addict. Many people with addictions complete programs without using the word "addict" to describe themselves, but these individuals often find themselves doing multiple stints in rehab.

The most effective method of addiction treatment involves a **multidisciplinary** approach—and it doesn't happen over night.

Detoxification

When a person decides to break free from addiction, the body must go through a process of withdrawal to rid itself of the toxic substances of the drug. Through a medically supervised process called detoxification, the individual goes

COUNSELING
SERVICES

Experts agree that the best way to tackle addiction is to combine education, counseling, medical treatment, and other approaches. Even then, it will be a long, slow process.

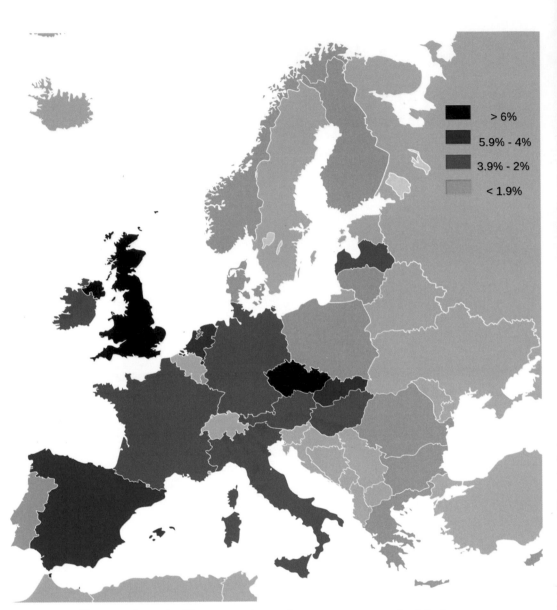

■	> 6%
■	5.9% - 4%
■	3.9% - 2%
■	< 1.9%

This map shows the lifetime prevalence of ecstasy use among all adults (ages 15 to 64 years old) in European nations. The European Union has taken a very different approach to ecstasy use from what the United States has. Instead of criminalizing ecstasy use or treating it as an illness, the EU uses a "harm reduction" policy that includes allowing users access to free pill-testing that will let them know exactly what they are consuming.

through some or all of the withdrawal symptoms specific to the substance of addiction. How long withdrawal lasts depends on how much and what type of drug was taken. Ecstasy withdrawal symptoms include fatigue, loss of appetite, depression or depressed feelings, and trouble concentrating.

After detoxification, a person with an ecstasy addiction needs follow-up treatment to prevent **relapse** and maintain sobriety. There are no specific treatments for ecstasy abuse and addiction. In general, the most effective treatments for drug abuse and addiction are cognitive-behavioral interventions that help change the patient's thinking, change behaviors related to his drug use, and increase stress-coping skills. Drug abuse recovery support groups may also be effective in combination with behavioral interventions to support long-term, drug-free

What Do Rehab Programs Accomplish?

Abstinence
In many cases it seems that as long as the substance is in the blood stream, thinking remains distorted. Often during the first days or weeks of total abstinence, we see a gradual clearing of thinking processes. This is a complex psychological and biological phenomenon, and is one of the elements that inpatient programs are able to provide by making sure the patient is fully detoxified and remains abstinent during his or her stay.

Removal of Denial
In some cases, when someone other than the patient, such as a parent, employer, or other authority, is convinced there is a problem, but the addict is not yet sure, voluntary attendance at a rehab program will provide enough clarification to remove this basic denial. Even those who are convinced they have a problem with substances usually don't admit to themselves or others the full extent of the addiction. Rehab uses group process to identify and help the individual to let go of these expectable forms of denial.

recovery. There are currently no pharmacological treatments for addiction to MDMA.

Behavioral Treatment Programs

Put simply, behavioral treatment programs teach people with addictions to change their behaviors so they are less likely to repeat those that led to addiction in the first place. Well, that's the theory anyway. Unfortunately, nothing about addiction is simple. Though behavioral treatment programs do help those with addictions find ways to avoid behaviors that can cause a relapse, they also must help them discover what led to those behaviors initially. Cognitive-behavioral therapy helps the individuals recognize how thought patterns influence behaviors. During therapy, individuals learn

Support groups are designed to give members a place where they can belong and draw strength from others who face problems similar to their own.

In the United Kingdom, the government is fighting addiction with education. FRANK is a drug education program that brings information to young adults across the UK.

how to change negative thought patterns, thereby changing behaviors. Individual and family therapy can help the person with addiction and those around her learn how to live as and with a recovering addict. Therapy can also help the addicted individual and her friends and family handle relapses; most people do relapse at some point during recovery.

Behavioral treatment programs also help those with addictions handle life without the drug, including the sometimes-painful cravings for the drug. If the individual is likely to encounter the drug in his daily life, he needs to know how to handle that situation to lessen the possibility that he will relapse. Otherwise, the likelihood of a successful recovery becomes less. No matter what substance was abused, the best treatment results are achieved when the individual practices *abstinence* from the substance.

Behavioral treatment programs often begin with a period of inpatient treatment. Depending on the length, severity, and drug of addiction, inpatient treatment can be short-term (usually a minimum of thirty days) or long-term residential. At first, some programs allow inpatients to have minimal—if any—contact with the "outside world." Patients concentrate on learning about themselves and their relationship with the drug. Later, family and perhaps close friends are encouraged to participate in the treatment program.

Support Groups

The individual fighting an addiction may feel as though she is the only person who has experienced what she's going through. Her addiction may have put a strain on her relationship with friends and relatives who don't use drugs. She may find it difficult to relate to anyone about how she's feeling. This is where a support group may be a valuable resource.

Alcoholics Anonymous

One of the best-known support groups is Alcoholics Anonymous (AA), founded in 1935 with the goal of helping people who have problems with alcohol. Today there are chapters all over the world. Its books and pamphlets are published in more than thirty languages.

Each chapter's program is based on the original twelve steps that have become synonymous with AA. The steps have a spiritual component, to which some people might object, but many studies have proven the value of some form of prayer and meditation to a recovery program. The AA program emphasizes that the Higher Power referred to in the steps does not refer to any particular belief system; it can mean what the individual wants—and needs—it to mean. The twelve steps are:

1. We admitted we were powerless over alcohol—that our lives had become unmanageable.
2. Came to believe that a Power greater than ourselves could restore us to sanity.
3. Made a decision to turn our will and our lives over to the care of God as we understand Him.
4. Made a searching and fearless moral inventory of ourselves.
5. Admitted to God, and to our selves, and to another human being the exact nature of our wrongs.
6. We're entirely ready to have God remove all these defects of character.
7. Humbly asked Him to remove our shortcomings.

Dr. Bob Smith, with the help of Bill Wilson, started Alcoholics Anonymous in 1935.

8. Made a list of all persons we had harmed, and became willing to make amends to them all.
9. Made direct amends to such people wherever possible, except when to do so would injure them or others.
10. Continued to take personal inventory and when we were wrong promptly admitted it.
11. Sought through prayer and meditation to improve our conscious contact with God as we understand Him, praying only for knowledge of His will for us and the power to carry that out.
12. Having had a spiritual awakening as the result of these steps, we tried to carry this message to drug addicts and to practice these principles in all our affairs.

AA recognizes the importance of family and friends to the person as she adjusts to life as a recovering alcoholic. Al-Anon and Alateen operate as support groups for friends and families, helping those involved with the recovering alcoholic deal with the changes as well as realize they are not alone on their journey.

The success of AA has led to the development of other twelve-step programs, including Narcotics Anonymous (NA) and Cocaine Anonymous (CA). All are based on the same premises as AA. Though participation in AA and other twelve-step program meetings will not guarantee a recovery free from temptation and relapse, it can play an important role in staying sober.

Other Support Groups

For whatever reason, some people don't find twelve-step programs helpful. There are many other support

God grant me the Serenity to accept the things I cannot change Courage to change the things I can and the Wisdom to know the difference

Belief in a "Higher Power" is an important part of Alcoholics Anonymous.

Groups like Alcoholics Anonymous are built around the principal that addiction is best treated with help from others who have faced the same problem.

groups in which they can participate. Many hospitals, treatment centers, community centers, and houses of worship offer support groups for individuals working on recovery. Most have a social hour following the meeting, giving people the opportunity to mingle and enjoy refreshments as well as learn how others are coping with recovery.

If someone is shy, uncomfortable talking in groups, ill, or without transportation, these support groups may not work for him. This is where the Internet can play a major role in the recovery process. There is an Internet mailing list, chat room, or group for almost anything anyone can imagine, and this includes recovery from addiction. However, always you use caution when giving out personal information. Though most people who participate in these groups and lists are just seeking information and support, there are some with motives not quite so innocent. Be careful about giving out personal information; in most cases, first names should be enough. Should you decide to meet someone in person, make sure the meeting takes place in a public location, preferably during the day, and ask if you can bring along a friend.

Regardless of whether a person attends an in-person support group or participates in a virtual one, care should also be used when assessing the information he gets from that group. What works for one person might not work for someone else.

Education

The best addiction prevention method is to not become addicted in the first place. Educators in many areas have gotten savvy about effective ways to educate students about drugs and their effects.

One of the best-known programs is D.A.R.E. (Drug Abuse Resistance Education). The D.A.R.E. program, which began in Los Angeles in 1983, aims at teaching students from kindergarten through twelfth grade how to avoid drugs and violence, as well as how to resist negative peer pressure. Eighty percent of U.S. school districts each year implement the program, which is led by a police officer. In recent years, some experts and researchers on drug abuse have questioned success rates claimed by the program. Criticism has centered around lack of follow-up as the students enter later grades. Despite these criticisms, the program has grown and now even includes interactive activities on its website.

Ad campaigns can also play a role in education. For example, anti-smoking campaigns have relied heavily on television spots. The first ads, paid for by the American Lung Association and the American Cancer Society, appeared on television by 1967. In 1999, tobacco companies got involved in television campaigns—though not exactly by choice. As part of the Master Settlement Agreement between the tobacco industry and attorneys general of forty-six states and five territories, the American Legacy Foundation was created to encourage children to never begin smoking and to help individuals who already did smoke quit. The tobacco industry contributes to Legacy, and Legacy in turn uses the funds it receives for a variety of anti-smoking campaigns, including television ads called "truth" ads.

Do the ads work? It appears they do—sometimes. According to a 2002 study published in the *American Journal of Public Health*, the ads produced by Legacy

These kids are taking part in a D.A.R.E. activity designed to help them never become addicted to drugs.

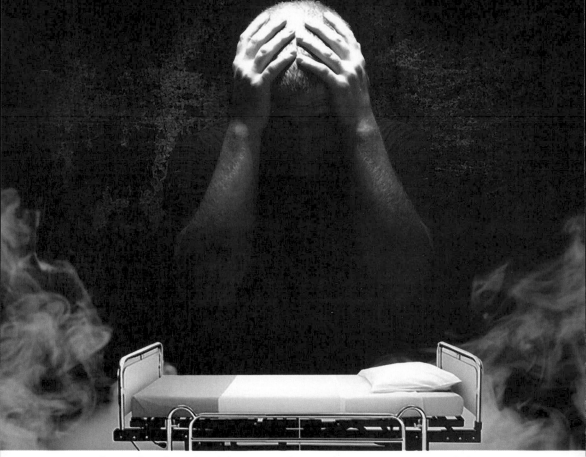

Researchers have found that some educational posters are not particularly effective.

reduced the number of children and teen smokers by 300,000. However, so-called truth ads created by tobacco company Philip Morris in a campaign called "Think. Don't Smoke" seemed to have had the opposite affect. Another article published in the *American Journal of Public Health*, this one in 2006, reported that the Morris campaign and others similar to it actually encouraged teens to smoke. Using data from Nielsen Media Research, researchers studied the impact of those ads on children and adolescents between the ages of twelve and seventeen in the seventy-five largest media markets in the United States. Melanie Wakefield, the study's head researcher, reported, "Tobacco-sponsored ads targeted at youth have no impact, and those targeted at parents seem to have an adverse effect on students who are in their middle and later teenage years." According to the researchers, these ads' purpose is not to prevent smoking but to merely delay it until the individual is an adult. In the end, researchers conclude, parents' influence is the most effective way to keep kids from smoking or doing other drugs.

But educational programs do not always have to come from adults and officials. Teenagers in Whitesburg, Kentucky, weren't willing to wait for adults to do something to convince children and other teens to stay off of OxyContin. Working with Appalshop, a cultural center, they produced a documentary about the perils of OxyContin abuse. The documentary, *Because of OxyContin*, featured real-life abusers of the drug telling personal stories of how abusing the drug affected their lives. Included in the documentary was a woman from southwest Virginia who blamed the drug for her losing a

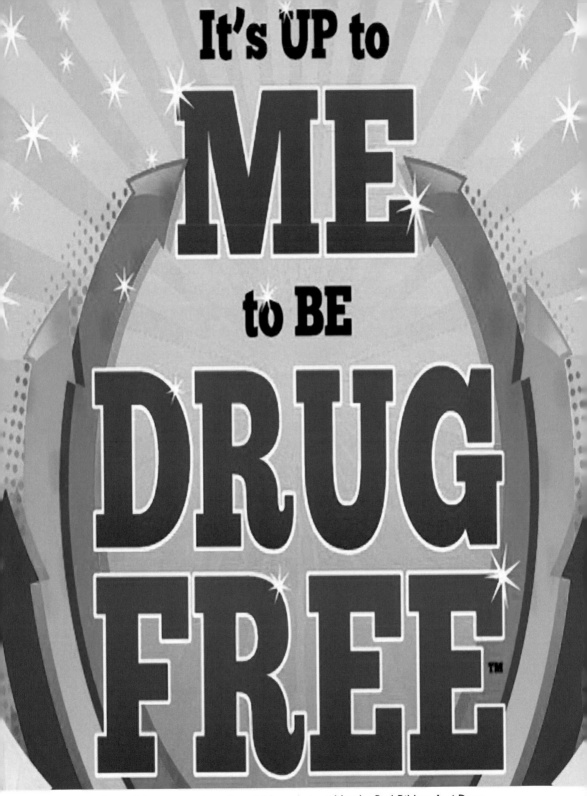

An anti-drug poster targeting children, designed by the Red Ribbon Anti-Drug Campaign.

child, contracting hepatitis, and possibly becoming infected with HIV.

Whatever its cause, whatever form it takes, and whatever methods are used to combat it, addiction affects everyone—it's everyone's problem, and everyone must be involved in the solution.

Remember Daniel from the beginning of the book? Here's what he'd like to tell other kids about drug abuse:

> I'd like to join an N.A. (Narcotics Anonymous) panel and talk to kids who are using. I'd tell them, Get out while you can. It starts out as all fun, games and parties but it leads to real nasty things. You become your own worst enemy.

Glossary

abstinence: The voluntary avoidance of something pleasurable that is harmful to you.

blood-brain barrier: A biological mechanism that keeps many substances from entering the blood vessels of the brain from the circulatory system.

clinical: A study carried out using careful scientific methods.

controversial: An issue about which people strongly disagree.

empathy: A feeling of emotional connection with other people.

hyperthermia: Abnormally high body temperature.

inhibitions: Feelings that make a person self-conscious and keep them from doing certain things.

innocuous: Something that is harmless and safe.

jurisdiction: The area where a set of laws apply.

metabolizes: Breaks down a substance so that it can be used by the body.

methamphetamine: A highly addictive stimulant drug sometimes known as "crystal meth" or "crank."

multidisciplinary: An approach to solving a problem using the expertise of several different fields, like medicine and psychology.

No Man's Land: In World War I, the unclaimed area between enemy lines where much of the fighting took place.

paranoid: Feelings of extreme fear and distrust of other people.

pharmacological: Having to do with the science of drugs including their chemistry, uses, and effects.

placebo: A treatment or drug given to a group within a medical study that doesn't have any actual physical effect.

post-traumatic stress disorder: Psychological problems caused by frightening, stressful, or violent events.

primordial: Something that has existed from the very beginning.

probation: A period of time during which a convicted criminal is under law enforcement supervision but is not in prison.

psychedelic: Creating hallucinations and altered states of consciousness.

psychoactive: Drugs that affect the human mind.

raves: Big dance parties with electronic music and light shows.

relapse: A return to drug use after a period of being off drugs.

synthesized: Created chemically in a laboratory.

therapeutic: Useful in the treatment of disease.

War on Drugs: The United States government's campaign to reduce the illegal drug trade.

Further Reading

Bankston, John. *Ecstasy =Busted.* Berkeley Heights, N.J.: Enslow Publishers, 2005.

Connolly, Sean. *Ecstasy: Straight Talking.* Philadelphia, Pa.: Saunders Book Company, 2009.

Elliot-Wright, Susan. *Amphetamines and Ecstasy.* Portsmouth, N.H.: Heinemann Library, 2005.

Esherick, Joan. *Dying for Acceptance: A Teen's Guide to Drug and Alcohol-Related Health Issues.* Broomall, Pa.: Mason Crest Publications, 2005.

Koellhoffer, Tara. *Ecstasy and Other Club Drugs.* New York: Chelsea House Publications, 2008.

Libal, Joyce. *Substance Related Disorders and Their Treatment.* Broomall, Pa.: Mason Crest Publications, 2004.

Marcovitz, Hal. *Club Drugs.* Farmington Hills, Mich.: Lucent Books, 2006.

Pilcher, Tim. *e, The Incredibly Strange History of Ecstasy.* Philadelphia, Pa.: Running Press, 2008.

For More Information

Club Drugs
www.nida.nih.gov/drugpages/clubdrugs.html

Drug Prevention Organizations
www.nationalfamilies.org/prevention/organization_index.html

Ecstasy and the Brain
faculty.washington.edu/chudler/mdma.html

History of MDMA (Ecstasy)
www.narconon.org/drug-information/ecstasy-history.html

National Institute on Drug Abuse
www.nida.nih.gov/NIDAHome.html

Partnership for a Drug-Free America
www.drugfree.org

The websites listed on this page were active at the time of publication. The publisher is not responsible for websites that have changed their addresses or discontinued operation since the date of publication. The publisher will review and update the website list upon each reprint.

Bibliography

About.com. "The Invention of MDMA or Ecstasy." inventors.about.
com/library/weekly/aa980311.htm (Accessed 13 December 2010)

Bennett, Drake. "Dr. Ecstasy," *The New York Times Magazine*, www.
nytimes.com/2005/01/30/magazine/30ECSTASY.html (Accessed 20
December 2010).

Brown, Ethan. "Professor X," *Wired*, www.wired.com/wired/ar-
chive/10.09/professorx.html?pg=1&topic=&topic_set=   (Accessed
21 December 2010).

Designer Drugs. "What Are Designer Drugs?" www.a1b2c3.com/
drugs/desi01.htm Accessed December 10, 2010.

Freudenmann, Roland W., Florian Öxler, and Sabine Bernschneider-
Reif. "The Origin of MDMA (ecstasy) revisited: the true story recon-
structed from the original documents." *Addiction History*, 101:1241–
1245.

Levin, Aaron. "Researchers Look to Ecstasy as PTSD Therapy Option,"
Psychiatric News, October 1, 2010, 45 (19): 26, pn.psychiatryonline.
org/content/45/19/26.1.full (Accessed 24 January 2011).

Nelson, Sheila. *Hallucinogens: Unreal Visions*. Broomall, PA: Mason
Crest, 2008.

NIDA. "MDMA (Ecstasy)." Abusedrugabuse.gov/ResearchReports/
MDMA/MDMA2.html#history (Accessed 13 December 2010).

NIDA. "The Brain: Understanding Neurobiology," science.educa-
tion.nih.gov/supplements/nih2/addiction/guide/lesson2-2.htm (Accessed 11 January 2011).

Narconon International. "History of Ecstasy (MDMA)," www.nar-
conon.org/drug-information/ecstasy-history.html (Accessed 13 December 2010).

Science Daily. "MDMA (Ecstasy)-Assisted Psychotherapy Relieves
Treatment-Resistant PTSD, Study Suggests," www.sciencedaily.com/
releases/2010/07/100719082927.htm (Accessed 26 January 2011).

Scientific American. "Self-Experimenters: Psychedelic Chemist Explores the Surreality of Inner Space, One Drug at a Time," www.scientificamerican.com/article.cfm?id=self-experimenter-chemist-explores-new-psychedelics (Accessed 21 December 2010).

Index

Picture Credits

Alcholics Anonymous: pp. 105, 107
Andreus: p. 48
Ashestosky: p. 108
Bouzou, Jean-Louis: p. 8
Czapnik, Sebastian: pp. 18, 23
Creative Commons: pp. 10, 13, 33, 40, 47, 56, 60, 90, 93
DEA: pp. 26, 78
Drozd, Mateusz: pp. 14, 17, 85
European Monitoring Centre for Drugs and Drug Addiction: p. 98
Ficara, John: p. 97
Kheng Ho To: p. 58
Kuzma: p. 21
Leeser: p. 55
MAPS: p. 69
Marchant, Xavier: p. 24

Author Biography

Malinda Miller is an author from upstate New York who has written several books for young adults.

Consultant Biography

Jack E. Henningfield, Ph.D., is a professor at the Johns Hopkins University School of Medicine, and he is also Vice President for Research and Health Policy at Pinney Associates, a consulting firm in Bethesda, Maryland, that specializes in science policy and regulatory issues concerning public health, medications development, and behavior-focused disease management. Dr. Henningfield has contributed information relating to addiction to numerous reports of the U.S. Surgeon General, the National Academy of Sciences, and the World Health Organization.